# MY FIRST
# PICTURE
# ATLAS

## illustrated by Jan Lewis
## and Clive Spong

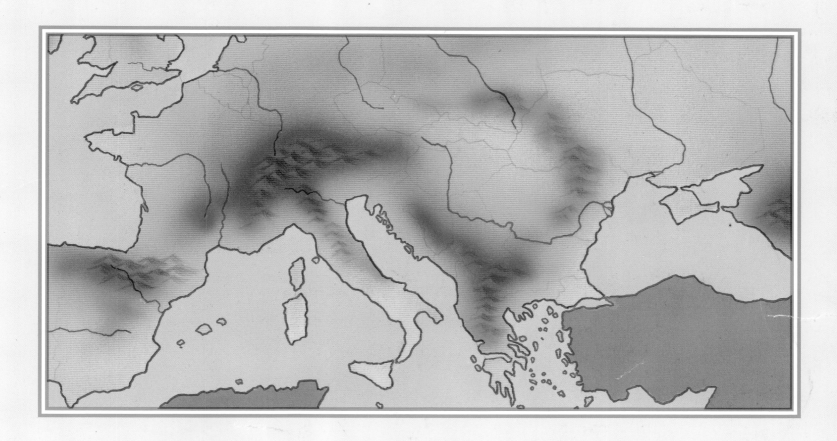

TS

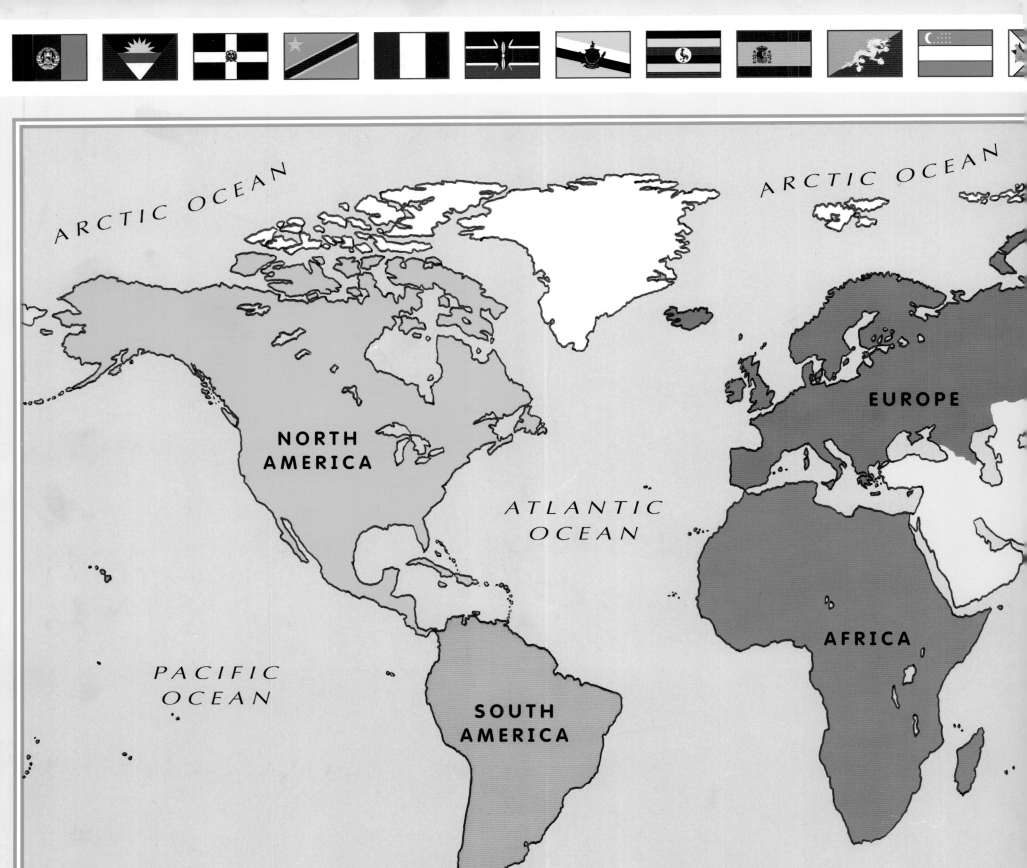

ARCTIC OCEAN

ARCTIC OCEAN

EUROPE

NORTH
AMERICA

ATLANTIC
OCEAN

AFRICA

PACIFIC
OCEAN

SOUTH
AMERICA

SOUTHERN

ANTARCTICA

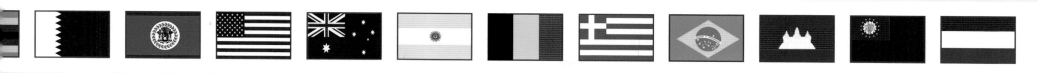

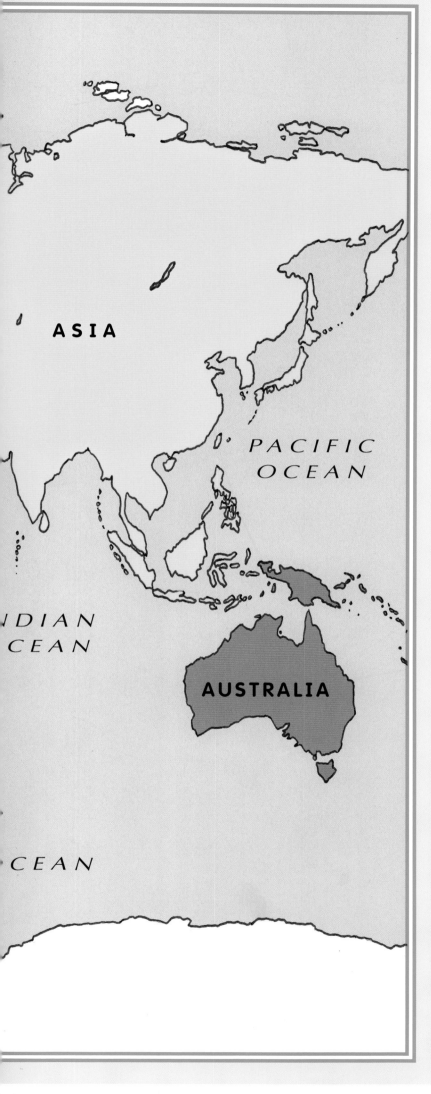

ASIA

PACIFIC
OCEAN

INDIAN
OCEAN

AUSTRALIA

OCEAN

# CONTENTS

# COUNTRIES OF NORTH AMERICA

 **CANADA**   **UNITED STATES**   **MEXICO**

*ARCTIC*

*BEAUFORT SEA*

**ALASKA**
*(USA)*

*Yukon*

*Mackenzie*

*BERING SEA*

**Anchorage**

**C A N A**

*GULF OF ALASKA*

*PACIFIC OCEAN*

**Vancouver**

Canada, the United States of America (USA), and Mexico make up the continent of North America. Canada is the most northerly country and the second largest in the world. The USA is mainly in central North America. Alaska, which is part of the USA, is in the far north, nearer Russia than the main part of the country. Mexico to the south borders Central America. About 450 million people live on this rich and powerful continent.

**U N I T**

**O F**

**San Francisco**

**Los Angeles**

## WHERE IN THE WORLD

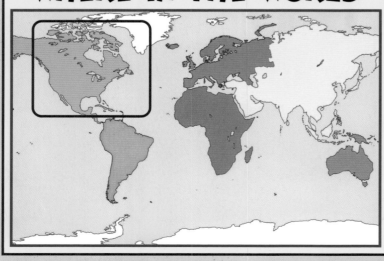

### MEXICO
*With over 100 million people, Mexico is a crowded country. More than half its people live in the cities. It also has beautiful beaches like this one stretching out to the Caribbean Sea.*

OCEAN

BAFFIN
BAY

LABRADOR SEA

HUDSON
BAY

DA

GREAT
LAKES

*Superior*

**OTTAWA** ■ ● **Montreal**

*Huron*

Gulf of
St. Lawrence

*Missouri*

D STATES

*Michigan*

**Toronto** ●

*Ontario*

*Erie*

ERICA

*Ohio*

● **New York**

*Mississippi*

■ **WASHINGTON DC**

ATLANTIC

OCEAN

GULF OF
MEXICO

MEXICO

■ **MEXICO CITY**

CARIBBEAN
SEA

## CN TOWER, TORONTO, CANADA
*This tower is one of the world's tallest structures. It has floors made of glass so you can see all the way down – over 550m (nearly 1800 ft)!*

## NEW YORK CITY, USA
*New York is both the largest city in the USA and a major international port. Its skyline is world famous. In the centre of the picture you can see the Empire State Building. It has 102 floors and is the city's tallest skyscraper.*

# WILDLIFE OF NORTH AMERICA

 right whale

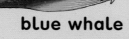 blue whale

 musk ox

husky dog

moose

bald eagle

ptarmigan

beaver

 grizzly bear

racoon

bighorn sheep

bobcat

North America is a continent of extremes. It has freezing temperatures and permanent ice in the north. In summer, deserts in the south-west become some of the hottest places on Earth. Between the mountain ranges that run down either side of the continent are great forests, lakes, grasslands, and deserts. In Mexico, you will find the most northerly rainforest in the world.

PACIFIC OCEAN

ROCKY MOUNTAINS

bottle-nosed dolphin

mountain lion

sea otter

pika

pelican

rattlesnake

## SONORAN DESERT
*Giant saguaro cactus grow up 13m (over 40 ft) high. They are native to this, one of the world's wettest deserts.*

## PRAIRIE LANDS
*Rich soil and hot summers make the flat lands in mid-west America ideal farmland. Maize is grown here.*

 sperm whale

8

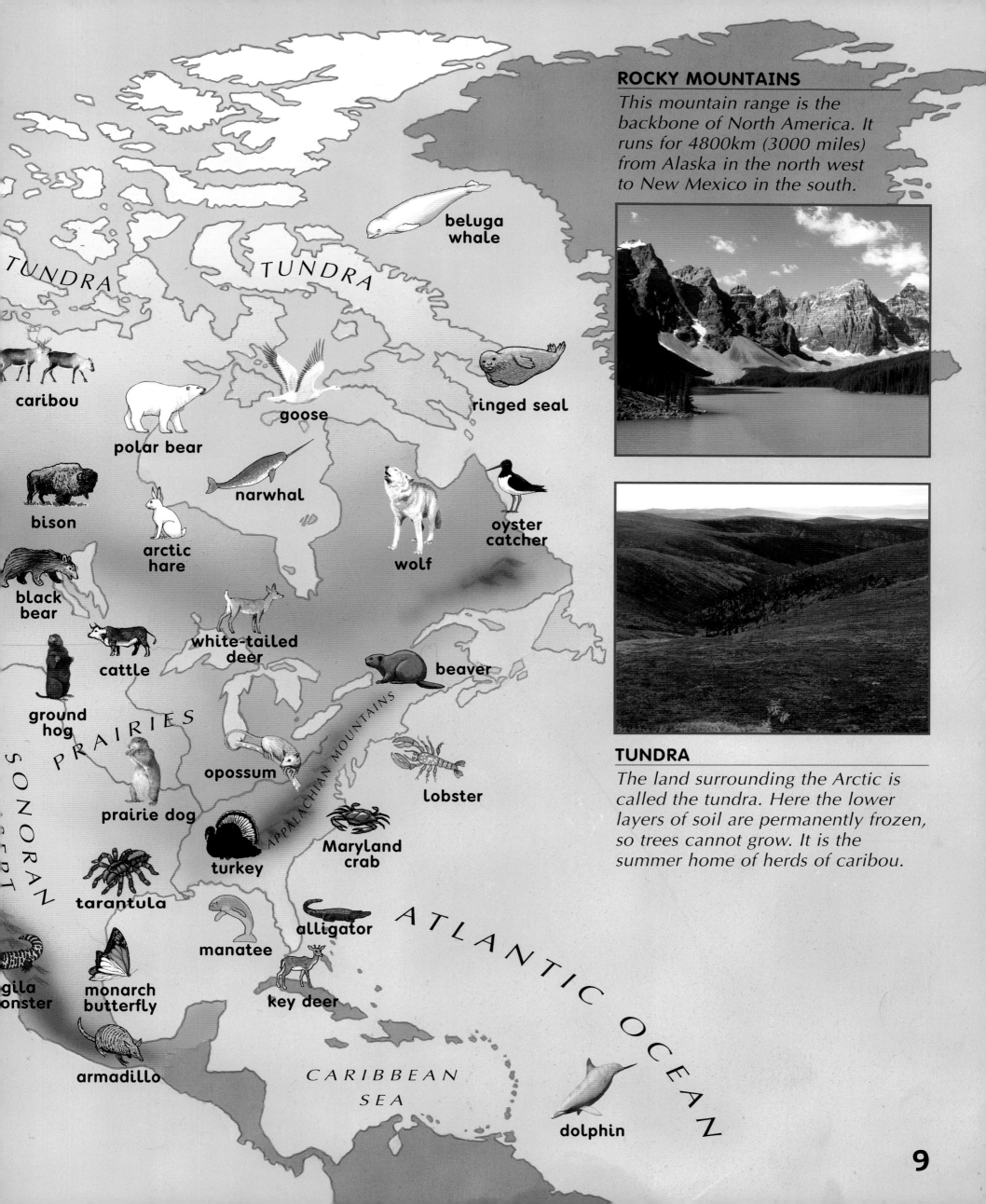

TUNDRA

TUNDRA

beluga whale

caribou

polar bear

goose

ringed seal

bison

narwhal

wolf

oyster catcher

arctic hare

black bear

cattle

white-tailed deer

beaver

ground hog

PRAIRIES

opossum

APPALACHIAN MOUNTAINS

lobster

SONORAN

prairie dog

turkey

Maryland crab

tarantula

manatee

alligator

gila monster

monarch butterfly

key deer

armadillo

CARIBBEAN SEA

ATLANTIC OCEAN

dolphin

## ROCKY MOUNTAINS

This mountain range is the backbone of North America. It runs for 4800km (3000 miles) from Alaska in the north west to New Mexico in the south.

## TUNDRA

The land surrounding the Arctic is called the tundra. Here the lower layers of soil are permanently frozen, so trees cannot grow. It is the summer home of herds of caribou.

**9**

# CENTRAL AMERICA

Seven small countries: Guatemala, Belize, Honduras, El Salvador, Nicaragua, Costa Rica and Panama, together with the islands that lie in the Caribbean Sea, make up Central America. This region joins the two great land masses of North and South America.

GULF OF MEXICO

HAVANA

CUB

turtles

angel fish

flying fish

CARIBBEAN SEA

dolphin

toucan

BELMOPAN

BELIZE

howler monkey

eagle

GUATEMALA

GUATEMALA CITY

red snapper

HONDURAS

TEGUCIGALPA

EL SALVADOR

SAN SALVADOR

macaw

NICARAGUA

tree frog

MANAGUA

blue morpho

barracuda

COSTA RICA

turtle

sloth

SAN JOSÉ

hummingbird

jaguar

Panama Canal

PANAMA

PANAMA CITY

fiddler crab

bottle-nosed dolphin

PACIFIC OCEAN

scorpion

GUATEMALA

EL SALVADOR

BELIZE

HONDURAS

NICARAGUA

COSTA RICA

PANAMA

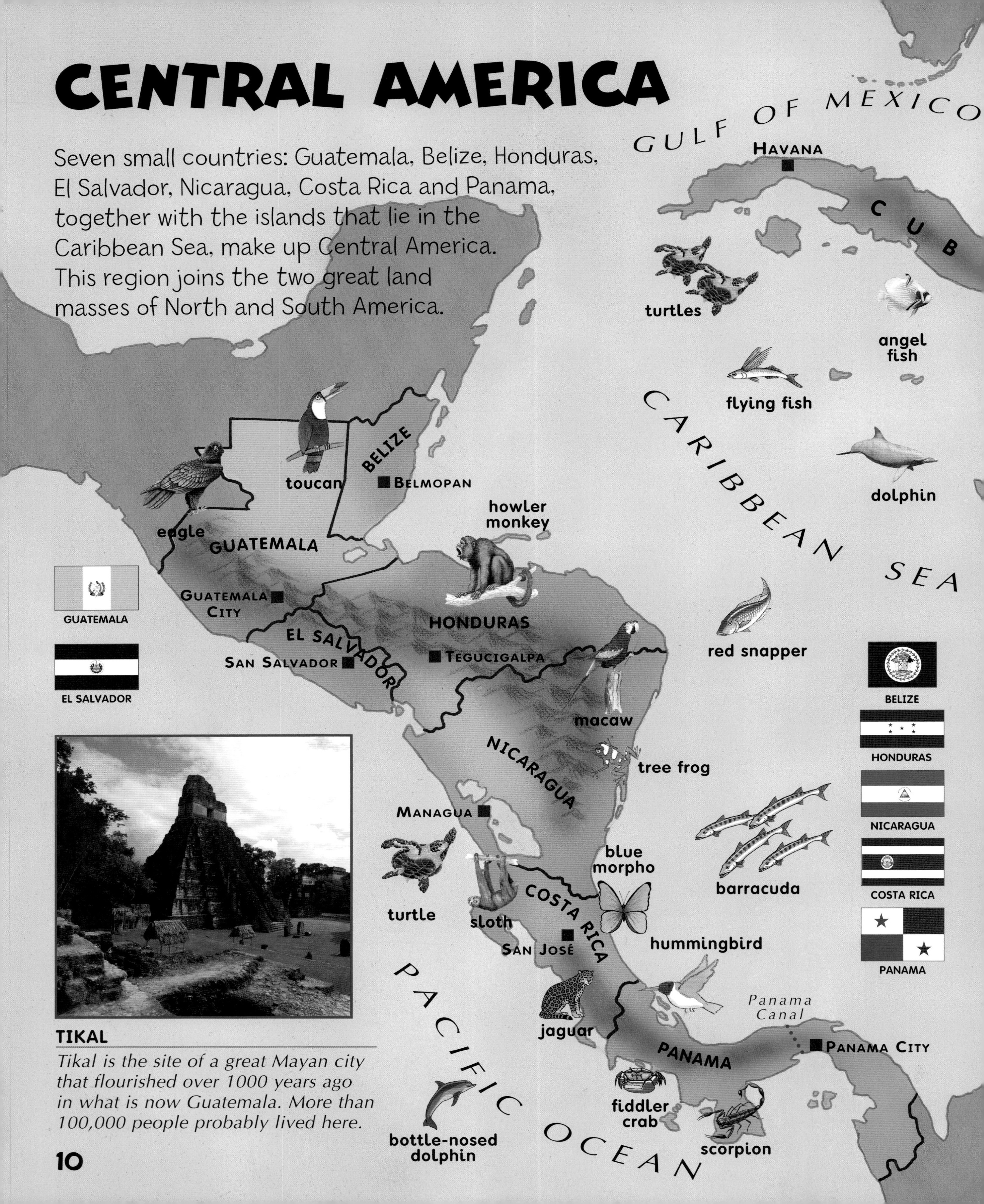

## TIKAL

*Tikal is the site of a great Mayan city that flourished over 1000 years ago in what is now Guatemala. More than 100,000 people probably lived here.*

BAHAMAS

ATLANTIC OCEAN

N

hummingbird

sea horse

TURKS & CAICOS ISLANDS

| BAHAMAS | CUBA | HAITI | DOMINICAN REPUBLIC | JAMAICA |
| PUERTO RICO | ST KITTS & NEVIS | ANTIGUA & BARBUDA | TURKS & CAICOS ISLANDS | DOMINICA |
| | GRENADA | ST LUCIA | BARBADOS | |
| | ST VINCENT & GRENADINES | TRINIDAD & TOBAGO | | |

JAMAICA

bat

HAITI

DOMINICAN REPUBLIC

starfish

flying fish

PUERTO RICO

## PANAMA CANAL

*This waterway was completed in 1914. It links the Pacific and Atlantic Oceans. Nearly 15,000 ships pass through it every year.*

## CARIBBEAN ISLANDS

*There are more than 7,000 islands stretching in a chain 4000km (2500 miles) long. Many have beautiful beaches like this.*

ST KITTS & NEVIS

ANTIGUA & BARBUDA

GUADELOUPE

red snapper

DOMINICA

MARTINIQUE

ST LUCIA

ST VINCENT & GRENADINES

GRENADA

BARBADOS

flying fish

TOBAGO

TRINIDAD

# COUNTRIES OF SOUTH AMERICA

There are 12 countries in South America. European explorers first came here in the 15th century and colonized much of the continent. Most of the 380 million people who live here today are of mixed European and Amerindian descent. Spanish is the most widely spoken language.

**MACHU PICCHU**

*Once a great Inca city, Machu Picchu was built in the mountains of Peru more than 500 years ago. It was abandoned less than 100 years later.*

CARIBBEAN SEA

CARACAS ■

VENEZ

BOGOTA ■

COLOMBIA

QUITO ■

ECUADOR

ANDES MOUNTAINS

PERU

LIMA ■

LA PAZ

B

PACIFIC OCEAN

CHILE

ANDES MOUNTAINS

SANTIAGO ■

ARGENTINA

VENEZUELA

COLOMBIA

GUYANA

SURINAME

BRAZIL

ECUADOR

PERU

BOLIVIA

CHILE

PARAGUAY

ARGENTINA

URUGUAY

Orinoco

GEORGETOWN

PARAMARIBO

CAYENNE

GUYANA

SURINAM

FRENCH GUIANA

Negro

Amazon

Madeira

Amazon

Tocantins

B R A Z I L

BRASILIA

San Francisco

IVIA

PARAGUAY

ASUNCIÓN

A

Parana

Parana

● Rio de Janeiro

● São Paulo

URUGUAY

MONTEVIDEO

BUENOS AIRES

N

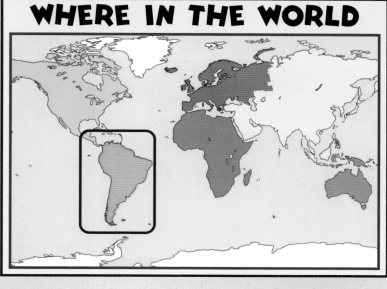

A T L A N T I C
O C E A N

## PAMPAS

In Argentina there are dry, grassy plains with few trees. They are called the pampas. Here, you will find vast cattle ranches. Cowboys, called gauchos, look after them.

## RIO DE JANEIRO

This city is famous for its carnival, beaches and giant statue of Jesus. Rio de Janeiro was once the capital of Brazil, South America's only Portuguese speaking country.

# WILDLIFE OF SOUTH AMERICA

Down the western side of the continent runs the Andes, the world's longest mountain chain. To the east of these mountains are the Amazon basin and rainforest in the north, rich grasslands in the middle, and cold barren lands to the far south. More different kinds of animals and plants live here than anywhere else on Earth.

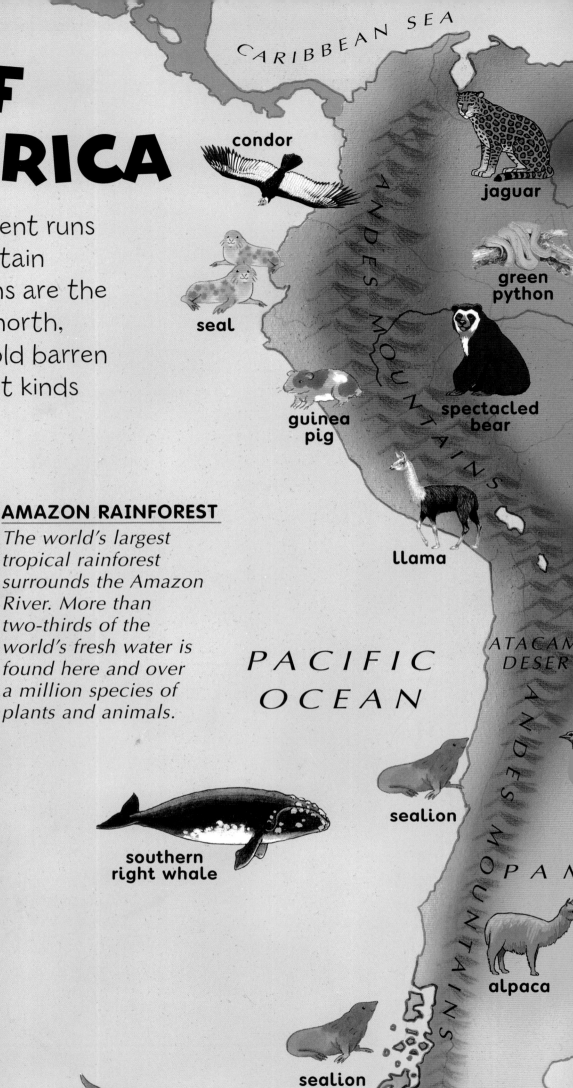

### AMAZON RAINFOREST
*The world's largest tropical rainforest surrounds the Amazon River. More than two-thirds of the world's fresh water is found here and over a million species of plants and animals.*

### ATACAMA DESERT
*This is the driest desert on Earth. Some parts have had no rain for over 400 years. Few plants or animals can live in this barren land.*

14

toucan

capybara

white shark

*AMAZON*

*RAINFOREST*

blue
morpho

tree frog

macaw

spider
monkey

sloth

peccary

howler
monkey

anteater

bat

tapir

hummingbird

armadillo

rhea

eagle

*A S*

pampas
cat

turtle

seagull

ephant seal

sperm whale

*ATLANTIC OCEAN*

## ANDES MOUNTAINS

*These mountains run the length of South America, more than 7000km (4000 miles). The lower slopes at the northern end of the chain are covered in grasses. Here live llamas, deer, bears and many birds including condors. In the colder south, there is little life.*

## IGUAZO FALLS

*On the border between Brazil and Argentina lie the Iguazo Falls. Here 275 separate waterfalls drop up to 82m (270 ft). Little can be heard above the roar of the water.*

**15**

# COUNTRIES OF AFRICA

There are 54 countries in Africa. About 800 million people live here, speaking more than 1,000 different languages. Africa is almost an island. It is joined to Asia by a narrow piece of land called the Sinai Peninsula.

MADEIRA

ALGIERS

RABAT · ATLAS MOUNTAINS · TUNIS · TUNISIA

MOROCCO

TRIPOLI

CANARY ISLANDS

ALGERIA

SAHARA

MAURITANIA

· NOUAKCHOTT

MALI

NIGER

CAPE VERDE ISLANDS

SENEGAL

DAKAR · GAMBIA

Niger

Lake Chad

BAMAKO ·

· NIAMEY

GUINEA BISSAU

BURKINA FASO

NIGERIA

GUINEA

CONAKRY ·

FREETOWN · SIERRA LEONE

IVORY COAST

GHANA

TOGO

BENIN

Niger

· ABUJA

MONROVIA · LIBERIA

YAMOUSSOUKRO

ACCRA

YAOUNDÉ · CAMEROON

EQUATORIAL GUINEA

LIBREVILLE · GABON

ATLANTIC OCEAN

BRAZZAVILLE

KINSHASA

LUANDA ·

MOROCCO

ALGERIA

TUNISIA

LIBYA

EGYPT

MAURITANIA

MALI

NIGER

CHAD

SUDAN

ERITREA

DJIBOUTI

ETHIOPIA

SOMALIA

SENEGAL

GAMBIA

GUINEA-BISSAU

GUINEA

SIERRA LEONE

LIBERIA

BURKINA FASO

IVORY COAST

GHANA

TOGO

BENIN

NIGERIA

CAMEROON

CENTRAL AFRICAN REPUBLIC

EQUATORIAL GUINEA

GABON

REPUBLIC OF CONGO

DEMOCRATIC REP CONGO

UGANDA

RWANDA

BURUNDI

KENYA

TANZANIA

ANGOLA

ZAMBIA

MALAWI

16

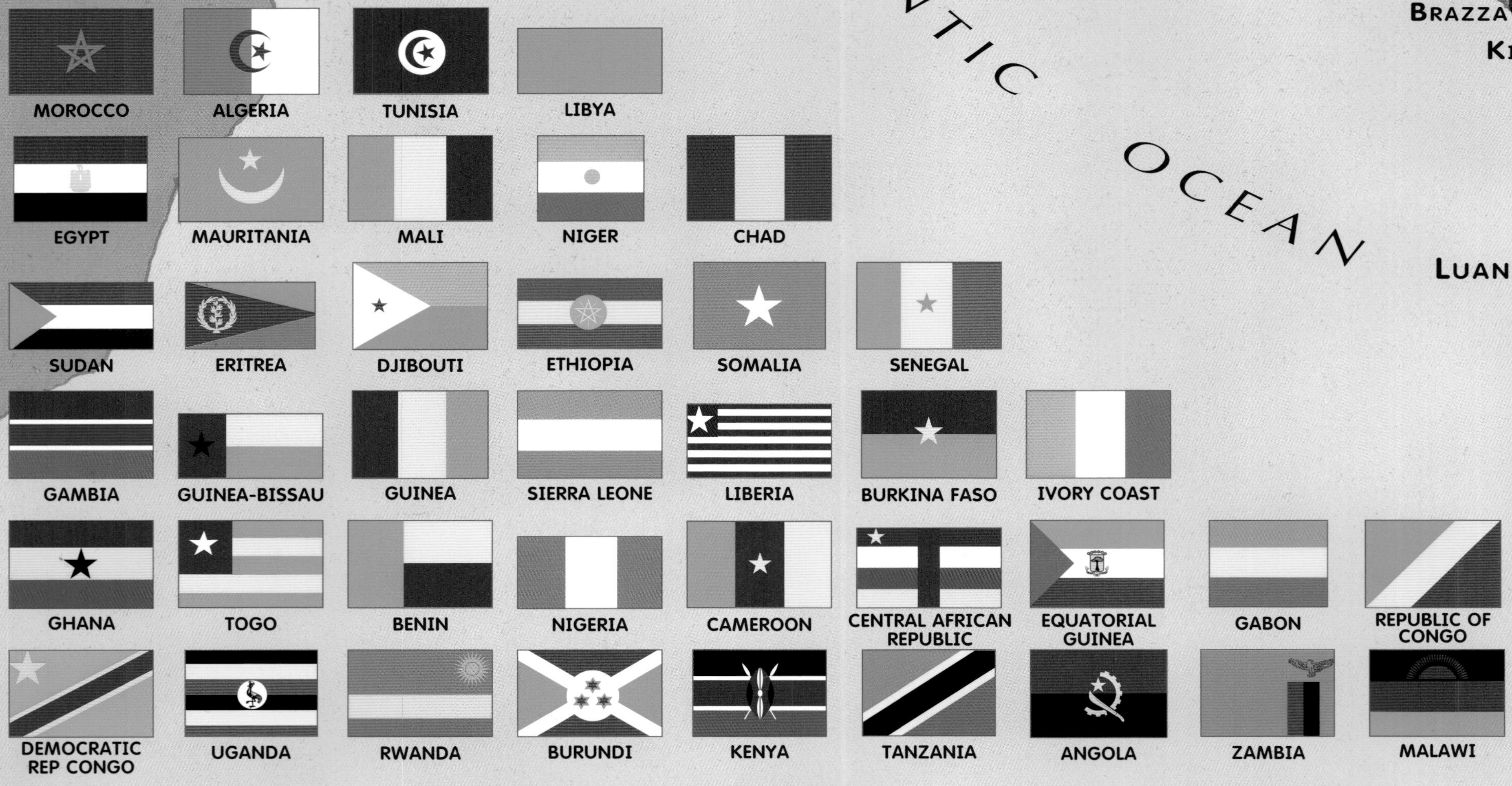

MEDITERRANEAN SEA

CAIRO ■ Sinai Peninsula

IBYA

DESERT EGYPT

Nile

RED SEA

CHAD

KHARTOUM ■ ASMARA ■ ERITREA

SUDAN DJIBOUTI

DJAMENA Nile ADDIS ABABA ■

NTRAL AFRICAN REPUBLIC ETHIOPIA

■ BANGUI SOMALIA

Congo Lake Turkana

DEMOCRATIC REPUBLIC OF THE CONGO

UGANDA KENYA

KAMPALA ■ ■ MOGADISHU

RWANDA Lake Victoria ■ NAIROBI

BURUNDI

TANZANIA

Lake Tanganyika ■ DAR ES SALAAM

NGOLA

ZAMBIA MALAWI

LUSAKA ■ ■ LILONGWE

Okavango Zambezi MADAGASCAR

HARARE ■ MOZAMBIQUE

NAMIBIA ZIMBABWE ■ ANTANANARIVO

WINDHOEK BOTSWANA

GABORONE ■ MAPUTO

PRETORIA ■ SWAZILAND

SOUTH AFRICA LESOTHO

■ Cape Town

## PYRAMIDS

These pyramids were built as tombs for the pharaohs, or rulers, in Ancient Egypt. They were built at Giza more than 4000 years ago.

## CAPE TOWN

Cape Town, South Africa's oldest city, is famous for its beautiful harbour and flat-topped Table Mountain.

ZIMBABWE    MOZAMBIQUE    MADAGASCAR    NAMIBIA

BOTSWANA    SWAZILAND    SOUTH AFRICA    LESOTHO

# WILDLIFE OF AFRICA

The north of Africa is dry and dusty desert and the sun is very hot. Camels and some antelope survive with little water but not many animals can live here. In central Africa there are steamy forests, large lakes and high mountains. Here you will find monkeys and gorillas, leopards and hippos, as well as lots of birds including pink flamingos. The grassy plains to the south are home to lions, elephants, giraffes, zebras, wildebeest, and hyenas.

## OKAVANGO DELTA

*The Okavango River flows inland and ends in Botswana, as the world's largest inland delta, or swamp. It provides much needed water to the area and is home to many animals like these hippos.*

18

## SAHARA DESERT

*This is the largest desert in the world; it is nearly as big as the USA! During the day this desert is so hot you can fry an egg under the sun. At night it is so cold water freezes.*

TERRANEAN SEA

RED SEA

INDIAN OCEAN

MADAGASCAR

**camel**

**crocodile**

**scorpion**

**hyena**

**hinoceros**

**elephant**

**hippo**

**vulture**

**turtles**

**gorilla**

**flamingo**

**zebra**

**frigate bird**

**wildebeest**

**snake**

**aardvark**

**giraffe**

**lion**

SAVANNA

**ppo**

**hyena**

**strich**

**cheetah**

**ring-tailed lemur**

**jellyfish**

## THE RIVER NILE

*The Nile is the world's longest river. It flows north from central Africa through to Egypt and out into the Mediterranean Sea, over 6500km (4000 miles)!*

## SAVANNA

*On these grasslands giraffe, zebra, wildebeest, and antelope graze. Lions hunt them for food. To protect these animals, large areas of Africa are now wildlife reserves.*

**19**

# COUNTRIES OF EUROPE

There are 48 countries in Europe; 27 of these form the European Union, which works to make it easier for countries to buy and sell products to each other. Russia and Turkey straddle the borders of Europe and Asia.

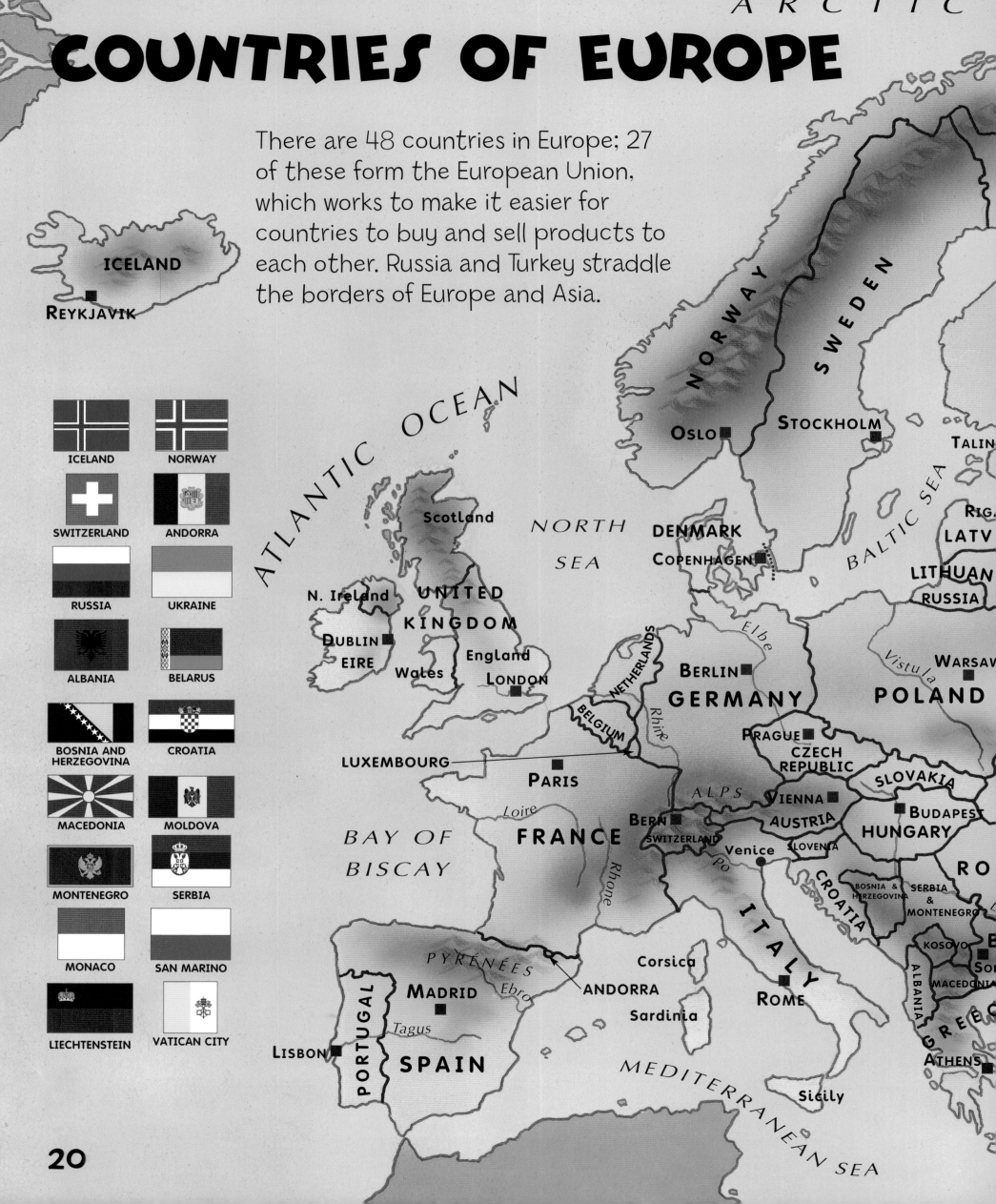

ICELAND

NORWAY

SWITZERLAND

ANDORRA

RUSSIA

UKRAINE

ALBANIA

BELARUS

BOSNIA AND HERZEGOVINA

CROATIA

MACEDONIA

MOLDOVA

MONTENEGRO

SERBIA

MONACO

SAN MARINO

LIECHTENSTEIN

VATICAN CITY

ICELAND

REYKJAVIK

ARCTIC

NORWAY

SWEDEN

OSLO

STOCKHOLM

TALIN

ATLANTIC OCEAN

NORTH SEA

BALTIC SEA

DENMARK

COPENHAGEN

RIG

LATV

LITHUAN

RUSSIA

Scotland

N. Ireland

UNITED KINGDOM

DUBLIN

EIRE

England

Wales

LONDON

NETHERLANDS

BELGIUM

Elbe

Rhine

BERLIN

GERMANY

Vistula

WARSAW

POLAND

PRAGUE

CZECH REPUBLIC

SLOVAKIA

LUXEMBOURG

PARIS

ALPS

VIENNA

AUSTRIA

BUDAPEST

HUNGARY

Loire

BERN

SWITZERLAND

Venice

Slovenia

BAY OF BISCAY

FRANCE

Rhône

Po

CROATIA

BOSNIA & HERZEGOVINA

SERBIA & MONTENEGRO

RO

PYRÉNÉES

Ebro

ANDORRA

Corsica

ITALY

KOSOVO

B

ALBANIA

MACEDONIA

So

PORTUGAL

MADRID

Tagus

ROME

Sardinia

GREE

Lisbon

SPAIN

MEDITERRANEAN SEA

Sicily

ATHENS

20

OCEAN

N

WHERE IN THE WORLD

FINLAND

Helsinki

RUSSIA

TONIA

Vilnius

Moscow

Minsk

BELARUS

Kiev

Dnieper

Volga

RAINE

MOLDOVA

Chisnau

NIA

Bucharest

BLACK
SEA

CASPIAN SEA

GARIA

Istanbul

TURKEY

NICOSIA
CYPRUS

## FLAGS OF COUNTRIES IN THE EUROPEAN UNION

| | | |
|---|---|---|
| BELGIUM | FRANCE | GERMANY |
| ITALY | LUXEMBOURG | NETHERLANDS |
| DENMARK | IRELAND | UK |
| GREECE | PORTUGAL | SPAIN |
| AUSTRIA | FINLAND | SWEDEN |
| CYPRUS | CZECH REPUBLIC | ESTONIA |
| HUNGARY | LATVIA | LITHUANIA |
| MALTA | POLAND | SLOVAKIA |
| SLOVENIA | BULGARIA | ROMANIA |

## VENICE, ITALY

*Venice is a beautiful city. It is built on water and has over 150 canals, 400 bridges, 3000 alleyways and no cars! To get around people walk, cycle, or take a boat ride.*

21

# WILDLIFE OF EUROPE

Two mountain ranges, the Alps and the Pyrenees, divide the continent into a cool, wet north and a warmer, drier south. The woodlands of central Europe are home to many animals. However, over 700 million people live in Europe and their cities, towns, and farms have destroyed many wild areas.

right whale

cod

puffins

reindee

ringed seal

snowy owl

NORWEGIAN SEA

eagle

oystercatcher

goose

seal

ATLANTIC OCEAN

cod

owl

wildcat

red squirrel

otter

mussels

pig

crab

humpback whale

puffins

badger

sheep

red fox

hedgehog

badger

bison

oysters

deer

snail

hare

clams

toad

wild boar

butterfly

woodpecker

dolphin

swordfish

lynx

brown bear

ADRIATIC SEA

rock goby

donkey

squid

donkey

scorpion

octopus

22

killer whale

tarantula

gecko

MEDITERRANEAN SEA

turtle

A R C T I C   O C E A N

blue whale

arctic fox

ringed seal

wolverine

Lemming

polar bear

brown bear

ptarmigan

lynx

wolf

reindeer

beaver

lynx

brown bear

saiga

owl

deer

wild horse

brown bear

otter

swans

bat

seals

BLACK SEA

CASPIAN SEA

grasshopper

tortoise

**FJORDS**

*Norway has hundreds of fjords along its western coastline. Fjords are deep bays formed by Ice Age glaciers tens of thousands of years ago.*

**TULIP FIELD, NETHERLANDS**

*Dutch flower bulbs are exported all over the world. The bulbs are first grown in large fields then harvested after flowering.*

**SUNNY SPAIN**

*Oranges, grapes, and olives thrive in the hot, dry summers and mild, wet winters of southern Europe.*

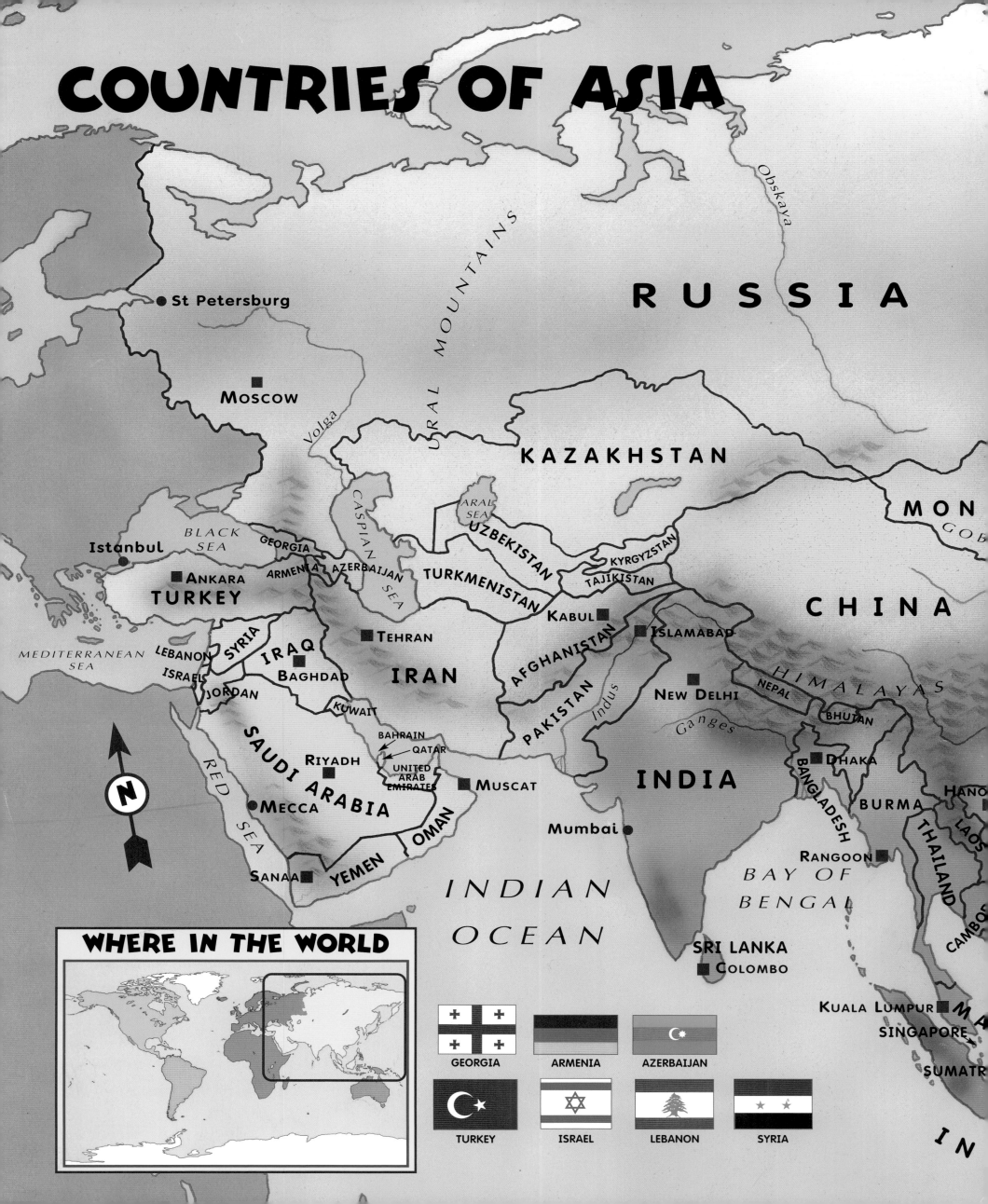

# COUNTRIES OF ASIA

St Petersburg

Moscow

Volga

URAL MOUNTAINS

Obskaya

**RUSSIA**

**KAZAKHSTAN**

ARAL SEA

**MON**

GOB

CASPIAN SEA

**UZBEKISTAN**

KYRGYZSTAN

TAJIKISTAN

**TURKMENISTAN**

GEORGIA

ARMENIA AZERBAIJAN

BLACK SEA

Istanbul

Ankara

**TURKEY**

MEDITERRANEAN SEA

LEBANON SYRIA

ISRAEL

JORDAN

**IRAQ**

Baghdad

Tehran

**IRAN**

Kabul

**AFGHANISTAN**

**PAKISTAN**

Indus

Islamabad

New Delhi

NEPAL

HIMALAYAS

BHUTAN

Ganges

**CHINA**

**INDIA**

Dhaka

BANGLADESH

HAN

**BURMA**

**MAL**

KUWAIT

BAHRAIN

QATAR

UNITED ARAB EMIRATES

**SAUDI ARABIA**

Riyadh

Mecca

RED SEA

Sanaa

**YEMEN**

**OMAN**

Muscat

**INDIAN OCEAN**

Mumbai

**BAY OF BENGAL**

Rangoon

THAILAND

LAOS

CAMBO

SRI LANKA

Colombo

Kuala Lumpur

SINGAPORE

SUMATR

IN

N

## WHERE IN THE WORLD

GEORGIA

ARMENIA

AZERBAIJAN

TURKEY

ISRAEL

LEBANON

SYRIA

## MOSCOW

*More than 10 million people live in Moscow, the Russian capital. The city has many fine buildings including St Basil's Cathedral, famous for its spires and domes.*

BERING SEA

ULAN BHATOR

LIA

DESERT

Vladivostock

BEIJING

Yellow

NORTH KOREA
Pyongyang

Seoul

SOUTH KOREA

JAPAN

Tokyo

Yangtse

Hong Kong

TAIPEI

TAIWAN

PACIFIC OCEAN

SOUTH CHINA SEA

MANILA

THE PHILIPPINES

BRUNEI

YSIA

BORNEO

CELEBES ISLANDS

JAKARTA

JAVA

ONESIA

EAST TIMOR

PAPUA NEW GUINEA

| | | | |
|---|---|---|---|
| RUSSIA | KAZAKHSTAN | MONGOLIA | UZBEKISTAN |
| TURKMENISTAN | IRAN | IRAQ | KYRGYZSTAN | TAJIKISTAN |
| AFGHANISTAN | PAKISTAN | CHINA | NORTH KOREA | SOUTH KOREA |
| JAPAN | JORDAN | SAUDI ARABIA | KUWAIT | BAHRAIN |

Asia is the largest continent. About 4 billion people live here. There are 50 countries or states in Asia; some, on the western border, have part of their land in Europe and part in Asia. One of these is Russia, the largest country in the world. It spans 11 times zones!

| | | | | |
|---|---|---|---|---|
| QATAR | UNITED ARAB EMIRATES | YEMEN | OMAN | INDIA |
| NEPAL | BHUTAN | BANGLADESH | BURMA | THAILAND |
| LAOS | CAMBODIA | SRI LANKA | VIETNAM | MALAYSIA |
| SINGAPORE | PHILIPPINES | BRUNEI | INDONESIA | EAST TIMOR |

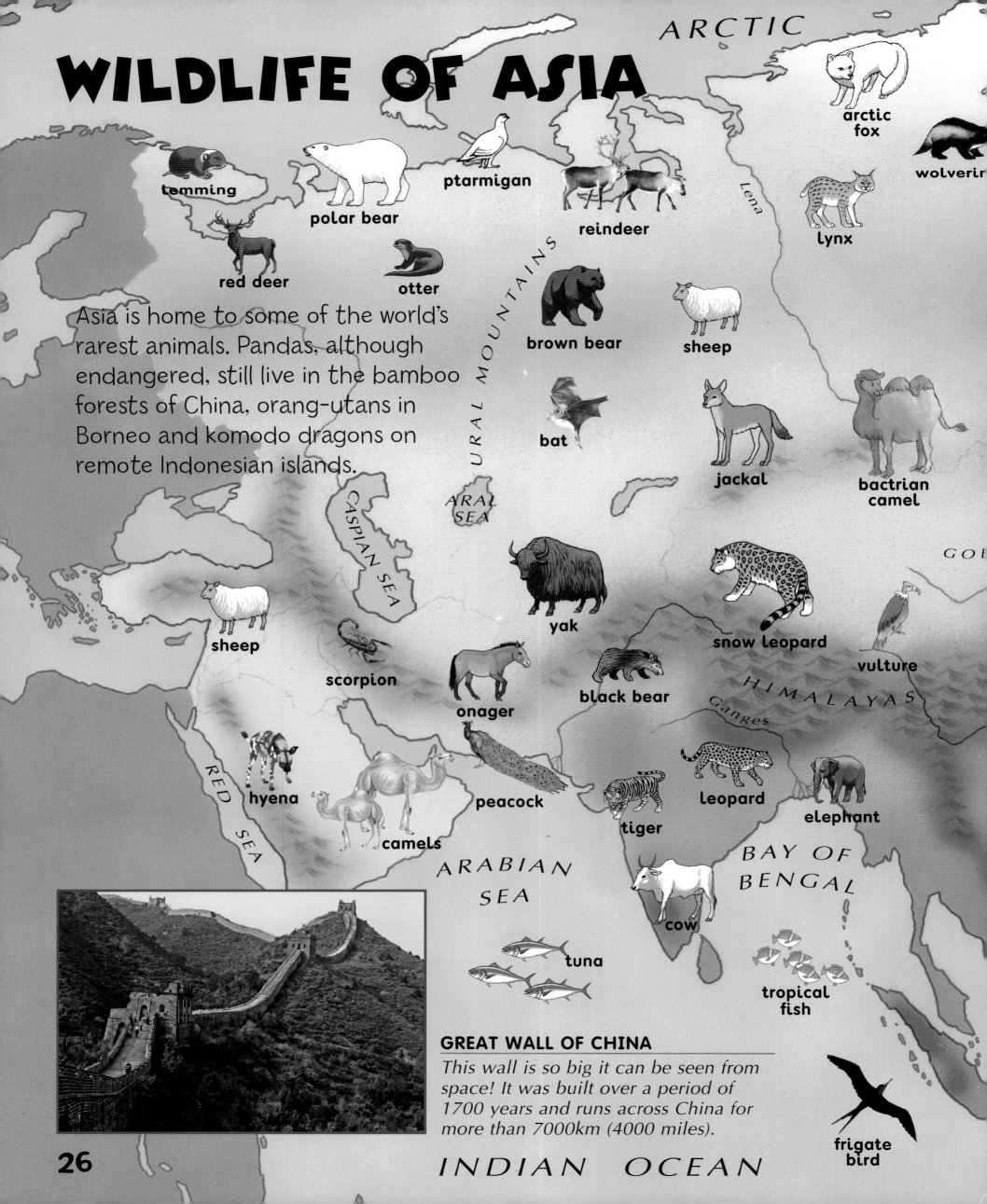

# WILDLIFE OF ASIA

ARCTIC

arctic fox

wolverine

lemming

polar bear

ptarmigan

reindeer

lynx

Lena

red deer

otter

brown bear

sheep

Asia is home to some of the world's rarest animals. Pandas, although endangered, still live in the bamboo forests of China, orang-utans in Borneo and komodo dragons on remote Indonesian islands.

URAL MOUNTAINS

bat

jackal

bactrian camel

ARAL SEA

CASPIAN SEA

GOBI

yak

snow leopard

vulture

sheep

scorpion

onager

black bear

HIMALAYAS

Ganges

hyena

camels

peacock

tiger

leopard

elephant

RED SEA

ARABIAN SEA

BAY OF BENGAL

cow

tuna

tropical fish

**GREAT WALL OF CHINA**

*This wall is so big it can be seen from space! It was built over a period of 1700 years and runs across China for more than 7000km (4000 miles).*

frigate bird

INDIAN OCEAN

# OCEAN

polar bear

walrus

humback whale

beluga whale

wolf

giant petrel

narwhal

bearded seal

...aiga

Siberian tiger

BERING SEA

cod

Yak

ringed seals

SEA OF OKHOTSK

...ESERT

puffins

squid

Yellow

...da

Yangtse

dugong

sea lions

PACIFIC OCEAN

SOUTH CHINA SEA

killer whales

orang utans

komodo dragon

giant clam

coral reef

## THE HIMALAYAS

The world's tallest mountain, Mount Everest, can be found in the Himalayas. It is 8850m (28,762 ft) high.

## GANGES RIVER

Every year many Hindu pilgrims visit the holy city of Varanasi to bathe in the Ganges River. Hindus believe this mighty river is sacred.

# AUSTRALIA AND NEW ZEALAND

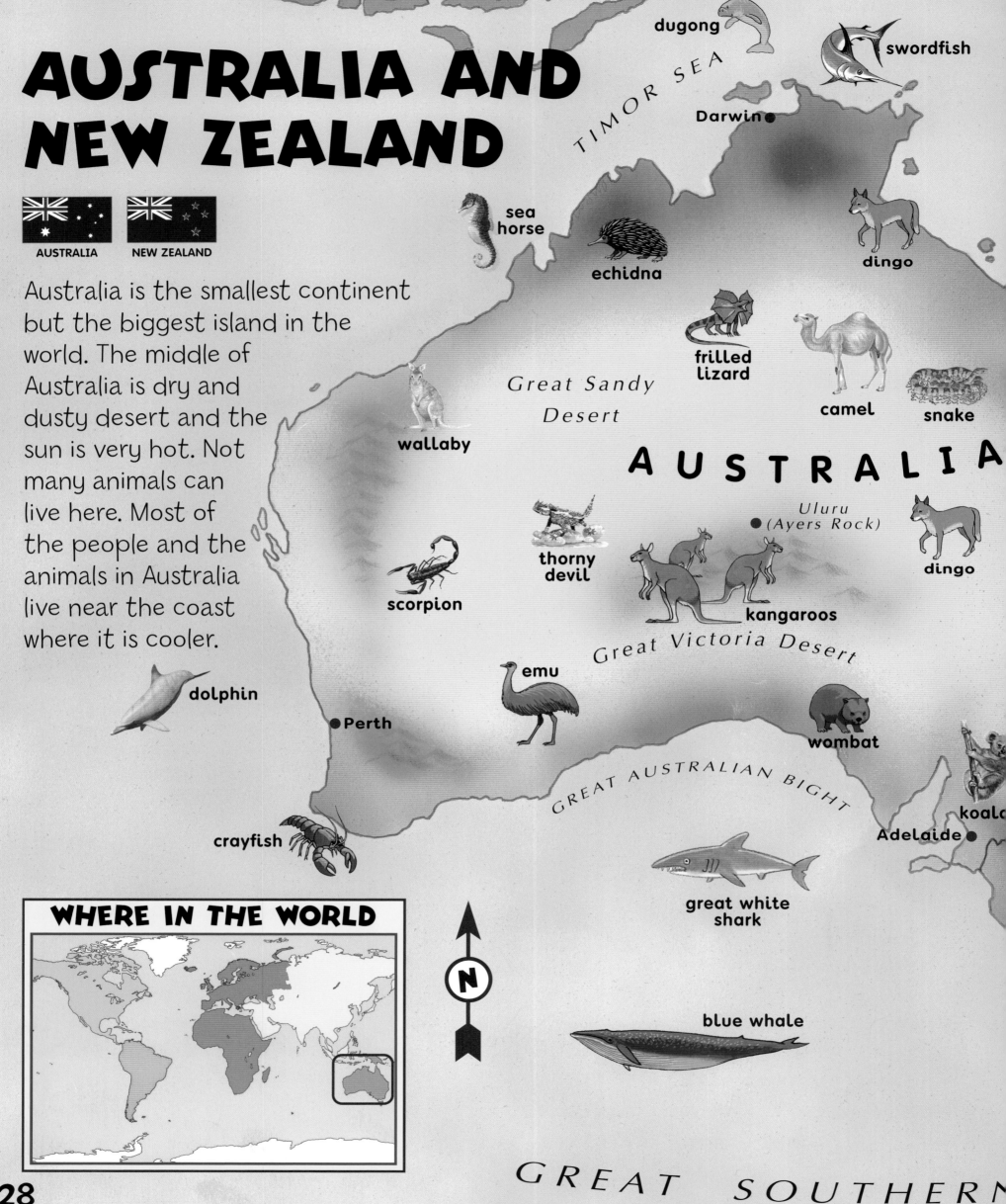

**AUSTRALIA**  **NEW ZEALAND**

Australia is the smallest continent but the biggest island in the world. The middle of Australia is dry and dusty desert and the sun is very hot. Not many animals can live here. Most of the people and the animals in Australia live near the coast where it is cooler.

dugong

swordfish

TIMOR SEA

Darwin

sea horse

echidna

dingo

frilled lizard

camel

snake

*Great Sandy Desert*

wallaby

A U S T R A L I A

*Uluru (Ayers Rock)*

thorny devil

scorpion

kangaroos

dingo

*Great Victoria Desert*

dolphin

emu

wombat

Perth

*GREAT AUSTRALIAN BIGHT*

koala

crayfish

Adelaide

great white shark

**WHERE IN THE WORLD**

N

blue whale

*GREAT SOUTHERN*

crocodile

tuna

flying
fish

GREAT

coral
reef

angel
fish

CORAL SEA

parrot
fish

bat

opossum

BARRIER

coral
reef

sea
horse

koala

kangaroo

platypus

REEF

coral
reef

Brisbane

sheep

*Darling*

platypus

Sydney

CANBERRA

turtle

red
snapper

Melbourne

TASMAN SEA

lionfish

albatross

great white
shark

Tasmanian
devil

TASMANIA

Hobart

killer
whale

OCEAN

Auckland

sealion

NEW ZEALAND

kiwi

tuatara

WELLINGTON

sheep

fur seal

penguin

elephant
seal

**ULURU (AYERS ROCK)**

*Every year up to half a million
people visit this gigantic red rock in
the desert centre of Australia. It is
sacred to the aboriginal people.*

**MILFORD SOUND**

*Mitre Mountain towers over this
beautiful fjord in New Zealand.*

# THE POLES

BERING
SEA

SEA
OF
OKHOTSK

killer
whale

cod

walrus

ALASKA
(USA)

bearded
seal

wolverine

wolf

beaver

wolf

moose

walrus

Siberian tiger

CANADA

polar bear

ARCTIC

snowy
owl

husky

salmon

OCEAN

narwhal

lynx

narwhal

*North*
⊙
*Pole*

RUSSIA

arctic
fox

arctic
hare

caribou

polar bear

reindeer

Canada
goose

GREENLAND

BARENTS
SEA

**ARCTIC OCEAN**

Nuuk
(Godthab)

musk ox

Lemming

*In northern Greenland,
a team of huskies pull this Inuit
hunter's sled across the frozen sea in
search of seals, walrus, and polar bears.*

ptarmigan

ICELAND

cod

ATLANTIC OCEAN

puffins

blue whale

The North Pole is
surrounded by the Arctic
Ocean. At the opposite side
of the world, the South Pole
is on Antarctica, a land that
is permanently frozen.

beaver

**30**